I LOVE PUPPIES, I LOVE DOGS

In memory of Pepper, Petey, Walter, Harley, and Bernice.
In Celebration of Jordy, Beau, Charlie, Bexley and Violet.

ISBN 978-0-578-71768-5

Noodle Nana

Big Book Love

a division of
www.swancygnet.com

Wiggly,
waggly,
jiggly,
jumpy

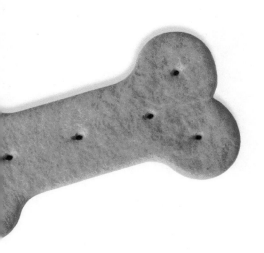

Shiny,
scruffy,
grinning,
grumpy

Yellow, black, white, red, or brown

Sitting up,
kerflopping
down

Long
and lean,
roly-poly

Stubby legs
plodding slowly

Sloppy kisses,
muddy paws

Floppy
ears
and
droopy
jaws

Pushed in noses
or great long snouts

Huge sled
pullers,
small snuggly
sprouts

Gruffy barkers,

Woeful
howlers,
feisty
yappers

Softball chasers,
frisbee catchers

Clever tricksters,
mitten snatchers

Chewing slippers,
chasing frogs